FEET AND SHOES

by

Toni Webber

Illustrations by

Carole Vincer

KENILWORTH PRESS

First published in Great Britain by
The Kenilworth Press Limited,
Addington, Buckingham, MK18 2JR

© The Kenilworth Press Limited 1990 and 1994

Reprinted 1991, 1993
Revised 1994

British Library Cataloguing in Publication Data
A catalogue record for this book is available from the British Library.

ISBN 1-872082-10-6

Printed in Great Britain by Westway Offset, Wembley

CONTENTS

Introduction

Every horse owner agrees that the foot is a vitally important part of a horse's anatomy. Injury of the foot can keep a horse out of work for months at a time. Horse-buyers ignore signs of foot problems at their peril. It is not for nothing that one of the best-known quotations in the horse world is 'No foot, no horse'.

The horse is a bulky animal which balances its weight on remarkably small feet and slender legs. The intricate structure of tissue and bone which makes up the legs not only has to support the bulk but also has to carry it, often at speed, over ground which may be rock-hard, squelchy with mud, rutted, bumpy or littered with stones.

For more than 2,000 years, horseshoes have been used to protect horses' feet from excessive wear, but the wall of the hoof is not the only part which can suffer from misuse; all parts play a role in keeping a horse sound. This book outlines the importance of a horse's foot and offers guidelines on its proper care, in particular how to recognise potential problems and how to prevent them from developing.

The horse in the wild

Wild horses do not have caring owners and skilled farriers to keep their feet in perfect condition. Yet the vast majority of horses living wild manage to survive many years without serious hoof problems. It is tempting to imagine that Nature, efficient enough when left to her own devices, could equally well take care of the feet of domesticated horses and ponies.

Unfortunately, humans ask horses to take part in activities that no wild horse would ever be expected to do – riding out, hunting, jumping, driving along tarmac roads, and often being required to stand in a stable for hours on end. Most of these activities put an unnatural strain on feet and legs. It is up to us to counteract ill-effects with all the means in our power.

Imagine a wild horse or pony, living in a herd and roaming at will over a wide-ranging territory; it follows the herd leader across many miles of varying terrain, rarely staying to graze for long in any one place and usually visiting a water source at least twice a day. Its hooves wear down at a rate roughly equal to the speed of growth, and its diet contains plenty of fibre and essential minerals to keep the horn strong.

A domesticated horse, on the other hand, leads a restricted life. Turned out, it is bounded by the limits of its field. In work, its exercise is likely to be partly on roads. Left unshod, particularly in a soft, moist climate, its feet wear down more quickly than they grow. When shod, the foot just keeps growing while the shoe wears down. Under these circumstances, the neglected hoof can develop many problems, becoming split or sore, and, in the worst cases, the toes can grow so long that they curl upwards and back.

The evolution of the foot

Some fifty million years ago, EOHIPPUS, the tiny 'dawn horse', ran on feet with toes. Its forefeet had four hooved toes, its hind feet three, and its weight was carried on a central pad. Several million years later, its descendant, MESOHIPPUS, had grown to twice the size. All its feet had three toes and the central toe was prominent.

Another ten million years passed, and the primitive horse became MERYCHIPPUS. It fed on grass rather than leaves, had emerged from the forest to the open plain, and its weight was carried on a single hoof, although two side toes were present.

PLIOHIPPUS, which lived ten million years ago, was the first single-toed horse. It roamed the plains and was able to graze freely and to run swiftly from its enemies. Traces of the side toes were present on either side of the cannon bone.

EQUUS CABALLUS, the present-day horse, has existed for nearly a million years. It is a one-toed creature, but, as shown opposite, the single toe has become an intricate part of the horse's anatomy.

The fleshy frog enables the weight of the horse to cause the hoof to spread and contract with each foot-fall. This absorbs jarring and helps blood circulation. The heel should *not* be lowered to keep the frog lightly in contact with the ground, as lowering the heel unbalances the foot and puts strain on the stay apparatus, and this can also lead to rotation of the pedal bone.

Insensitive horn surrounds the hoof, growing downwards from the coronary band to protect the sensitive tissue inside the foot. It is thick enough to have nails driven through it without causing it to split, and it can be cut and trimmed just as our own nails can.

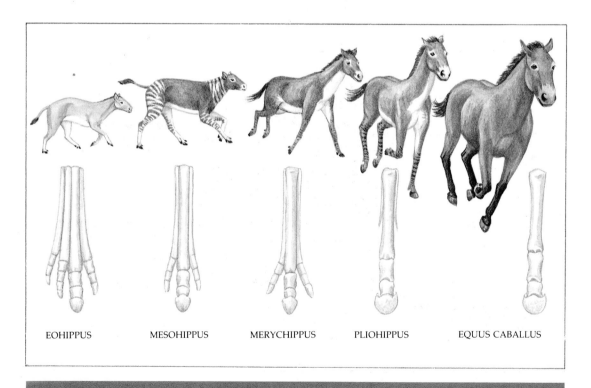

EOHIPPUS   MESOHIPPUS   MERYCHIPPUS   PLIOHIPPUS   EQUUS CABALLUS

SECTION THROUGH CENTRE OF FOOT

LONG PASTERN BONE

SHORT PASTERN BONE

CORONARY BAND – from which the horn grows

PERIOPLE – membrane of soft horn which controls evaporation

SENSITIVE LAMINAE – layers of fleshy tissue

HORNY LAMINAE – insensitive layers of horn lining the wall

WALL

DEEP FLEXOR TENDON – fibrous, elastic 'rope' which controls the foot's movement

NAVICULAR BONE – small bone to the rear of the pedal bone

WHITE LINE

PLANTAR or DIGITAL CUSHION – combines with the frog to prevent jarring

PEDAL BONE or THIRD PHALANX – the principal bone of the foot

UNDERSIDE OF THE FOOT

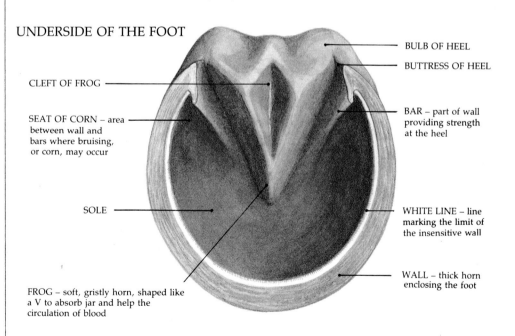

BULB OF HEEL

BUTTRESS OF HEEL

CLEFT OF FROG

SEAT OF CORN – area between wall and bars where bruising, or corn, may occur

BAR – part of wall providing strength at the heel

SOLE

WHITE LINE – line marking the limit of the insensitive wall

WALL – thick horn enclosing the foot

FROG – soft, gristly horn, shaped like a V to absorb jar and help the circulation of blood

Variations in the foot

Few horses and ponies have perfect conformation. Sometimes, faults are related: a heavy head and low head carriage may lead to a poor gait; light quarters may put extra strain on the hocks; a narrow body may cause the legs to brush against one another when the horse moves at speed.

The ideal shape and position of the foot, as shown below, should, however, be borne in mind when you are looking for a horse to buy. The reason, of course, is that the nearer a horse comes to perfection in the feet, the fewer problems are likely to arise when the horse is being ridden or used in competition and has the weight of a rider on its back.

Nevertheless, there is no need to reject a horse simply because its feet are not perfect, unless you intend to take part in showing classes. Most faults in the feet can be minimised.

Many horses have 'boxy' feet; others have broad, flat feet; and some have feet that turn in or out.

As long as you have a good farrier who understands the problems that can arise, much can be done by careful trimming of the foot and by sensible shoeing. It is often a good idea to consult a reputable farrier when buying a horse.

Where possible, the slope of the pastern if carried through the hoof to its junction with the ground should form an angle of 45-50 degrees to the ground. This slope should be parallel with the slope of the shoulder. Similarly, an imaginary vertical line up the centre of the leg from the bulbs of the heel should run through the shoulder to the crest.

Boxy feet are often allied to upright pasterns; flat feet to excessively sloping pasterns. In both cases, special shoes can help to counteract the effect.

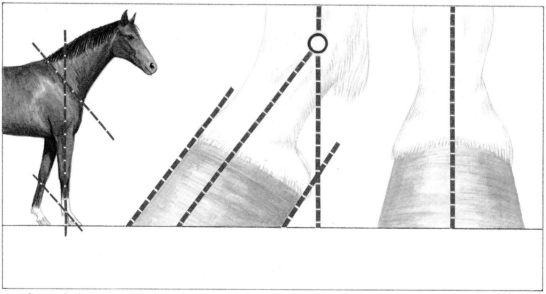

Angles with the ground, formed by a **normal foot**. From the side, the slope of the shoulder should match the slope of the foot and pastern (the foot-pastern axis or FPA).

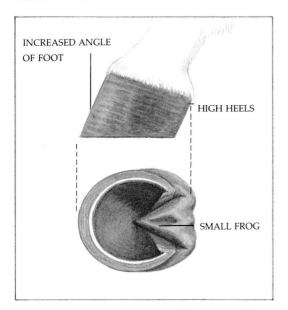

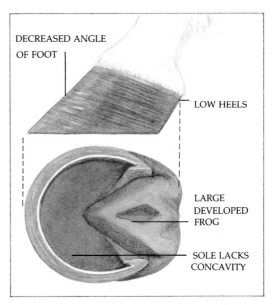

Boxy feet have short toes and form a wider angle with the ground. The small frog and contracted heels can cause concussion to the joints.

Flat, sloping feet have a shallower angle, causing tendon strain. The sole may lack concavity, which can lead to cracked toes and bruising.

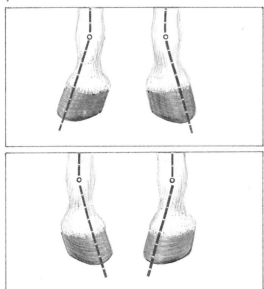

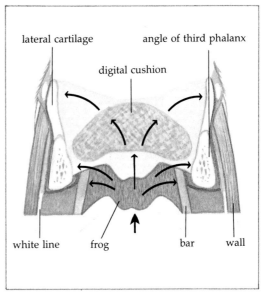

Toes which turn **out** (*top*) or **in** (pigeon-toes) are often allied to narrow or wide chests. Both kinds of feet cause uneven wear to the shoes.

This diagram shows how the weight of the horse causes the foot to expand in the direction of the arrows, thus **absorbing jarring** as foot meets ground.

The unshod foot

If a horse or pony is not doing much roadwork, is it really necessary for it to wear shoes? The answer depends mainly on the type of hooves it has.

Shoes are not essential if the feet are well shaped and tough, with strong horn and good frogs, and if the animal plants its feet squarely and straight. Another factor is where the horse lives and the work it has to do. If you have little roadwork and can ride over soft, springy turf, your horse's hooves will need little protection.

There are definite advantages in keeping your horse unshod: for example, costs are greatly reduced, although you will still require regular visits from the farrier to maintain the shape and condition of the hooves.

Where a number of horses are turned out together, unshod feet are likely to be safer, and a troublemaker in the field is less likely to cause damage to its companions. At a Pony Club camp, for instance, where ponies are turned out together at night, the organisers normally request owners to have the ponies' hind shoes removed.

Horses which are to be turned away for any length of time are usually best left unshod, so that the hoof can grow without any damage from nails. Nevertheless, the feet should always be inspected daily and trimmed as necessary. Regular attention, even when the horse is not working, is needed to keep the feet well shaped and healthy.

Grass tips are now obsolete. The purpose of these small half shoes was to prevent the toe from splitting, but they can cause sole bruising and the mechanical and circulatory problems which result from lowered heels.

Where horses are worked mainly on soft ground – a field or all-weather school – they can be ridden **without shoes**. The feet must be trimmed regularly.

If kicking occurs among field-kept ponies, unshod feet cause less damage. **Grass tips** are now obsolete.

The foot and breeds

The strength of the foot is related to the thickness of the horn. Also, some breeds have harder horn.

Generally speaking, horses from the hot, dry, desert regions of the Middle East, where grazing is poor, have naturally harder-wearing feet than horses of the wetter, lusher areas further north. It was the Celtic people in these areas, in pre-Christian times, who invented nailed-on metal shoes to protect the hooves.

The thicker the shell of the hoof, the more durable it tends to be. The panel on the right grades (from top to bottom) the thickness and strength of a horse's hoof according to its breed. It is, however, only a generalisation, and there is no guarantee that because your horse is an Arab it will have better hooves than your friend's Thoroughbred, and you should not plan your horse's hoof-care with this in mind.

Some people believe that a dark hoof is stronger than a pale one. The **colour** is due to pigmentation, and other experts think it has little effect.

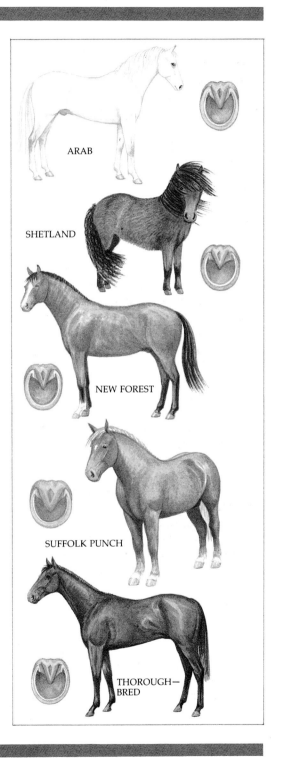

ARAB

SHETLAND

NEW FOREST

SUFFOLK PUNCH

THOROUGH—BRED

The farrier

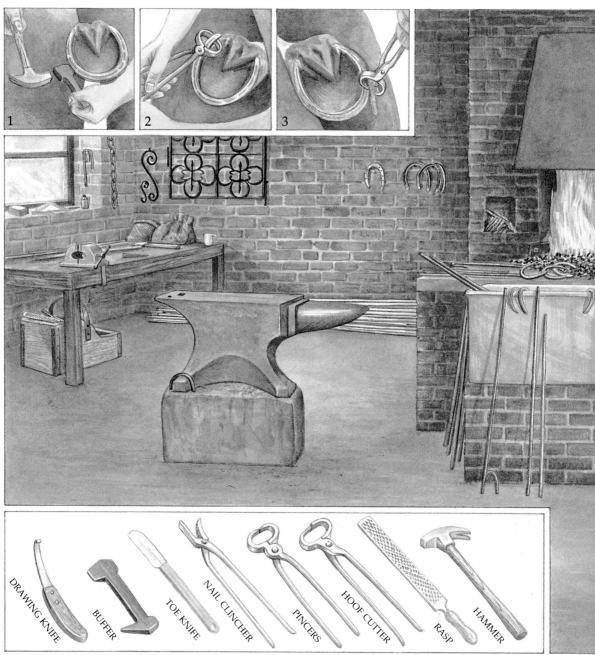

DRAWING KNIFE · **BUFFER** · **TOE KNIFE** · **NAIL CLINCHER** · **PINCERS** · **HOOF CUTTER** · **RASP** · **HAMMER**

1. Cutting off the clenches with **hammer** and **buffer**. 2. Using the **pincers** to lever off the old shoe. 3. The **hoof cutter** trims excess growth of horn to reveal the white line. 4. The **rasp** levels the surface of the foot to receive the shoe. 5. Trying on the **hot shoe** for

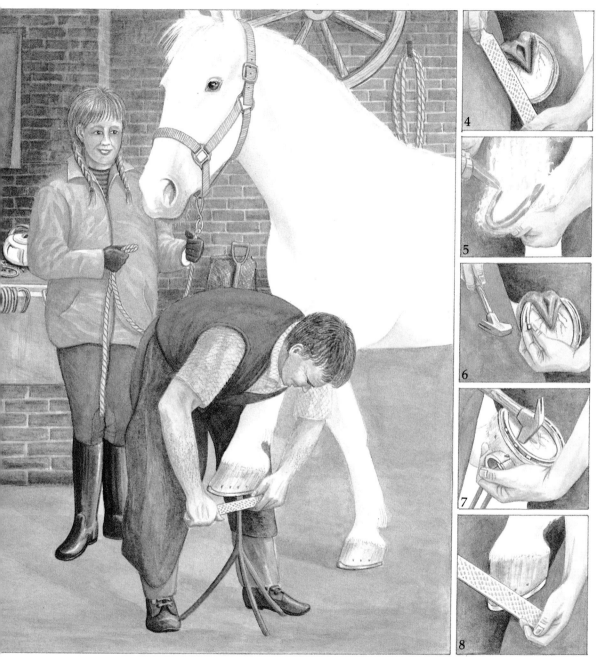

size. The charring indicates adjustments to be made to shoe or foot. 6. The **nails** must be angled correctly. 7. The emerging **nail tip** is twisted off and bent down to form the **clench**. 8. The foot is finished off by **rasping** below the line of clenches.

Shoes past and present

A horseshoe needs to be kept firmly in place, and the most efficient means of achieving this is to use nails. The Celts, who were skilled ironworkers, discovered that it was possible to secure shoes on a horse's foot by driving nails into the insensitive area of the hoof.

In the Middle East and around the Mediterranean, the hard-hooved Arab horses needed little protection. But a form of iron sandal, secured by thongs, was used by the Romans; the Greeks preferred a sandal made from woven grass. Neither of these 'sandals' could have been intended for regular use as it would have been difficult to prevent the foot from slipping or from collecting grit between shoe and sole. They were no doubt a form of remedial shoeing.

In Britain the nailed shoe continued to be in general use throughout the centuries. Usually it was made of plain iron, sometimes fitted with calkins (one or both branches of the shoe turned over to form a wedge or stud) to give better grip. Later 'fullered', or grooved, steel became the accepted material for shoes. Clips – to ensure a more secure fit – became a regular part of shoe design about one hundred years ago.

Shoes today may vary in design and material but this is for a specific reason. Remedial shoeing can help to reduce strain to ligaments and tendons caused by poor conformation. It can also minimise the effect of an injury, and aid healing processes by protecting or padding sensitive areas.

Lightweight aluminium and, most recent of all, plastic shoes are fitted to racehorses to prevent them from being impeded in a race by having to wear heavy shoes.

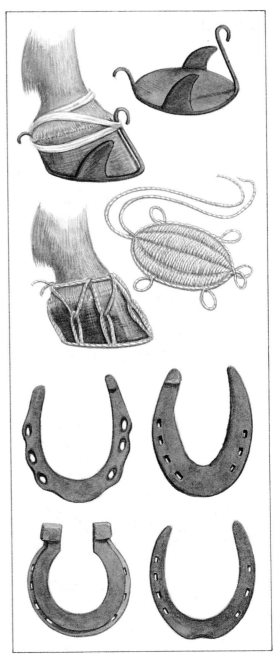

Ancient horseshoes: hippo-sandals in iron (Roman) and woven grass (Greek). **Nailed shoes**: (*from left*) mediaeval, Tudor/Stuart, key-hole, 19th century.

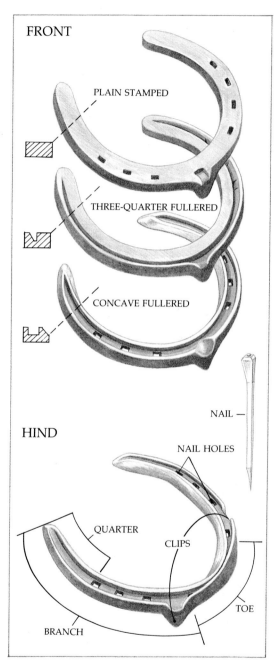

FRONT

PLAIN STAMPED

THREE-QUARTER FULLERED

CONCAVE FULLERED

NAIL —

HIND

NAIL HOLES

QUARTER

CLIPS

TOE

BRANCH

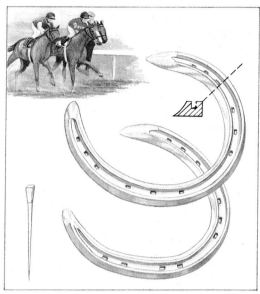

Racing plates in lightweight aluminium with slim nail and no clips. These shoes are worn only for racing, and in heavy going may be sucked off by mud.

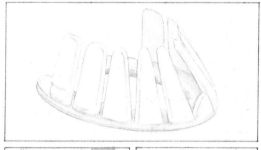

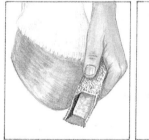

Horseshoes of the present. *Top*, front shoes in **plain iron**, **three-quarter fullered** and **concave fullered**. *Bottom*, hind shoe showing the different parts.

Plastic shoes for racehorses. Like the hippo-sandal of the past, the shoe fits around the foot. The hoof wall is sandpapered and the shoe glued in place.

Studs and their use

There are two basic types of stud in general use: road studs, or nails, set permanently into the shoes, for roadwork; and screw-in studs, which come in many different shapes and sizes, and are fitted when the ground is slippery.

The **road stud** is plug-shaped and tipped with hard-wearing tungsten carbide. Usually, it is fitted by the farrier into a specially made hole in the heels of each hind shoe. **Road nails** are cheaper, but the tungsten tips may not last the life of the shoes. Studs or nails should protrude as little as possible, to minimise the effect on the balance of the foot.

Screw-in studs *must be removed* as soon as the horse has competed. The holes in the heels of the shoes, usually just the hinds, are threaded and are plugged with cotton wool when not in use.

Studs are occasionally used in front shoes.

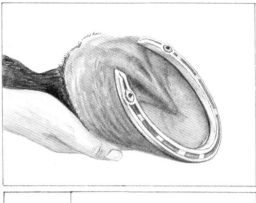

To upset the balance of the foot as little as possible, two studs or nails are better than one, and they should protrude by only a small amount.

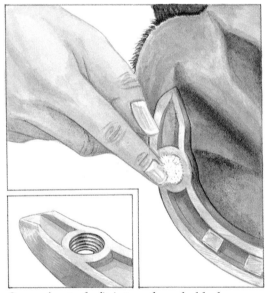

Screw-in studs fit into a threaded hole stamped into the heel of the hind shoe. The hole should be packed with tow or cotton wool when not in use.

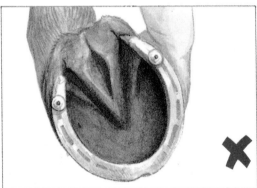

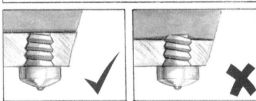

Top: Take care not to use screw-in studs on a **worn shoe**, for fear of damaging the foot. As shoes wear down *(bottom)*, so, of course, does the depth of the hole for the stud.

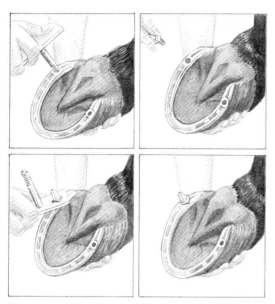

Remove packing, then clean out the hole with a **T-tap.** Insert the stud again and tighten it with the **T-tap spanner.**

Screw-in studs can be used for roadwork but only if they are designed for the purpose. The screw-in stud is short and blunt and has a carbon tip.

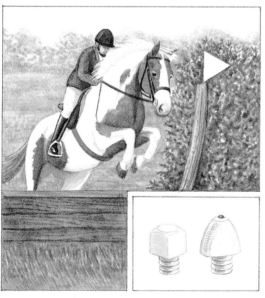

Standard studs are widely available and used for many activities, both flatwork and jumping. Remember to ask your farrier to make shoes with stud holes.

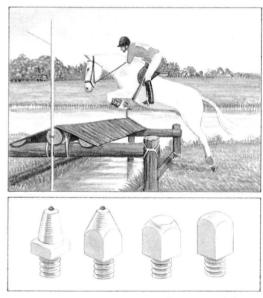

Choice of stud depends on the state of the ground. In dry, hard conditions, **pointed studs** should be used. Large **square studs** give extra grip in mud.

Care of the foot

With a stabled horse, the care of its feet is straightforward. Picking out the feet and checking the shoes become part of the regular daily routine and are not likely to be overlooked.

The same regular care is needed with horses at grass, but since they may not be ridden every day it is much easier to forget.

General care means picking out the feet, thoroughly cleaning the base of the foot, using a hoof-pick to remove dirt and small stones; checking for cuts and tender areas; feeling for heat in the fetlock and hoof wall and for any filling around the pastern; inspecting the state of the shoe and calling in the farrier before the shoe is completely worn out.

If the hoof is brittle or cracked, special supplements may be added to the diet to encourage the development of strong horn.

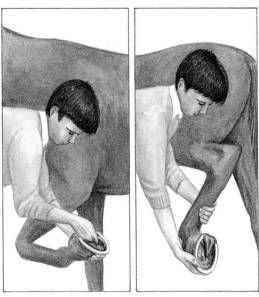

When **handling the feet**, stand facing the rear. Support the weight with one hand while examining hoof and sole, and lower gently to the ground afterwards.

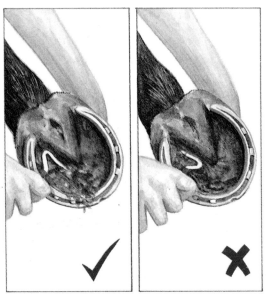

Use a **hoof-pick** to clean debris from the sole and around the frog. Always work the hoof-pick away from you for fear of damaging sensitive tissue.

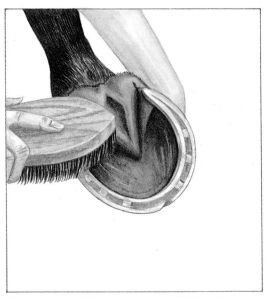

Once most of the compacted dirt has been removed, clean up the sole with a **water brush.** Be sure to dry heels thoroughly when you have finished.

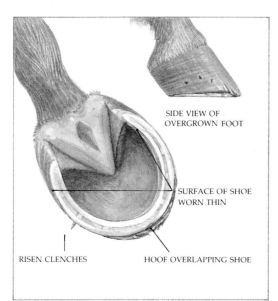

SIDE VIEW OF
OVERGROWN FOOT

SURFACE OF SHOE
WORN THIN

RISEN CLENCHES

HOOF OVERLAPPING SHOE

Look for **signs that a horse needs shoeing:** foot long, with horn growing over the shoe, shoe worn or distorted, nails loose and clenches risen.

At a show **hoof oil** adds the finishing touch. Do not use it daily as it can prevent water from being absorbed and will make the horn brittle.

Products containing **amino acids** help to promote healthy horn. **Bran**, which has a high phosphorus content, is detrimental, while **linseed oil** and **vitamins** have little

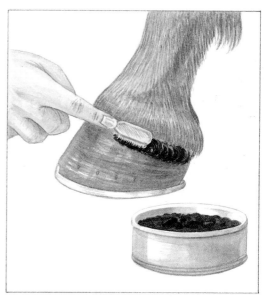

effect. Signs of a poor diet are **ridges** on the wall. **Special paste** can be smeared on the coronary band to enhance growth.

Conformation problems and cures

Like humans, many horses walk awkwardly because of poor conformation. At faster paces, or if the horse is tired, the fault is exaggerated and can cause injury when one foot strikes another.

Sometimes the inside edge of a front shoe hits the opposite leg. If the damage is near the knee, the action is known as 'speedy cutting'. Near the fetlock, it is 'brushing'.

'Over-reaching' occurs when the toe of the hind shoe strikes the heel or back of the foreleg. This is most likely to happen when a horse is jumping or galloping.

Imperfect action can also lead to uneven wear on the shoes – or in the case of 'forging' – to a shoe being pulled off by being trodden on.

In most cases, however, special shoeing will minimise problems.

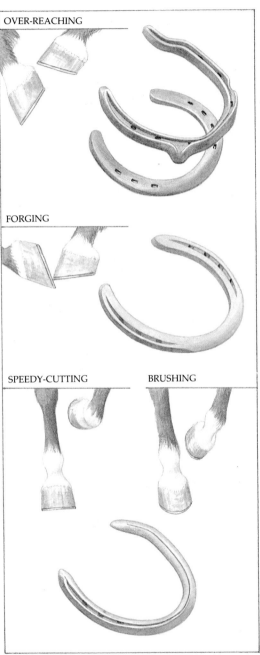

OVER-REACHING

FORGING

SPEEDY-CUTTING

BRUSHING

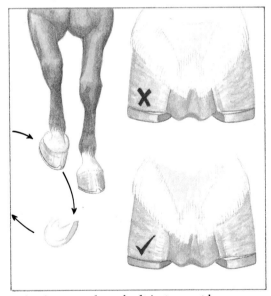

Winging may be a fault in toe-out horses. The foot swings in an inward circle. Shoes need lowering on inside edge.

Over-reaching – needs a shoe with rolled toe and long heel; **forging** – use dub-toed hind shoe; **speedy-cutting/brushing** – shoes need short, narrow inner branches.

20

Faults in shoeing

Standards in the shoeing of horses have greatly improved in recent years and most farriers have a profound knowledge of the anatomy of the foot and the problems that can occur. Nevertheless, there may still be a few unskilled farriers around and you should be able to recognise poor work. Remember that normally the shoe should be made to fit the foot.

When the foot is being prepared, the bearing surface should be made level. The toe must not be shortened by rasping (dumping). Neither frog nor sole should be pared; the bars should not be cut away.

With the shoe in place, the toe clip on the front foot should be centred. The heels must not be too short or too long. Clenches must be flush with the wall, the nailheads emerging in an even line. There should be no rasping of the hoof wall above the clenches.

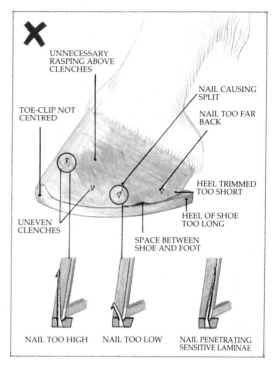

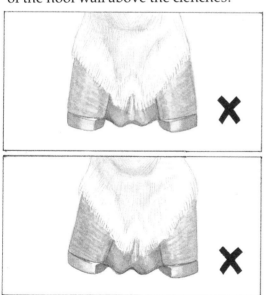

Poorly made shoes and **badly prepared feet**. *Top*: the frog does not touch the ground. *Bottom*: the shoe is uneven and the foot is crooked and not square.

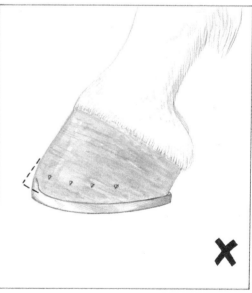

Dumping, in which the foot is shortened to match an ill-fitting shoe by rasping the toe, is a serious fault and can result in brittle feet.

21

Problems with the foot

In dry weather, particularly if the horn is brittle, the foot may develop cracks.

The **grasscrack** (also called 'false sandcrack') is a split travelling upwards from the ground. It is the least serious as long as it is dealt with promptly, by being cut away.

More serious is the **sandcrack,** running downwards from the coronary band. The cause, an unlevel or unbalanced hoof, must be treated, and the crack may then be riveted or a groove burned across it.

In **seedy toe** a cavity is formed by the separation of sensitive and insensitive laminae at the toe. The cavity must be cleaned and packed with Stockholm tar and cotton wool. The cause may be imbalance due to poor anterior/posterior foot preparation, laminitis or degenerative joint disease. Excessive tension on the deep digital flexor tendon can cause the pedal bone to rotate.

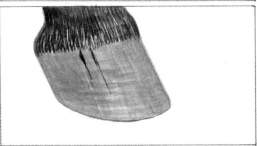

There are two types of crack. The **grasscrack** *(top)* may develop in over-long feet. The **sandcrack** *(bottom)* is more serious and harder to treat.

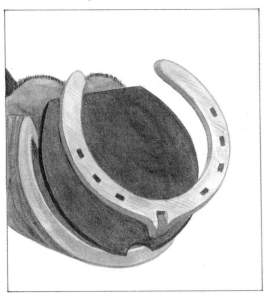

A **leather pad**, shaped to the foot, may be placed between shoe and foot to protect bruised or punctured soles where infection has developed.

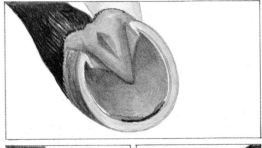

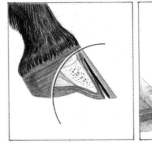

Seedy toe is a separation of the hoof wall from the insensitive lining in the toe area. To prevent infection, pack with Stockholm tar and cotton wool.

The sole of the foot can be quite sensitive and may be bruised or cut if the pony treads on a hard object.

A **bruise** may show as a reddish mark on the sole, noticeable only when the area is washed clean or if the pony flinches when the sole is tapped. A few days' rest usually cures the problem, although poulticing may be needed in severe cases.

A **corn** is a bruise in the angle between the wall of the hoof and the bar, usually caused by infrequent or inadequate shoeing. Treat as for a bruised sole and call in the farrier and the vet.

If the cleft of the frog is blackened and gives off a foul-smelling discharge, the horse is almost certainly suffering from **thrush.** This is due to bad management. Forcing the pony to stand in a dirty, wet stable and failing to clean out the feet regularly may cause the frog to degenerate so badly that thrush develops. Treatment consists of cutting away the rotten parts of the frog, applying antiseptic powder or a mild antiseptic solution and supplying the pony with clean, dry bedding.

The most likely cause of sudden lameness, especially when out for a ride, is that the horse has picked up a stone or other sharp object which has become lodged between the shoe and the frog. The stone can be seen as soon as the foot is picked up and, provided it is removed immediately, the horse should go sound again. For this reason, always carry a hoofpick in your pocket, especially out hacking. It is impossible to remove a firmly lodged stone with your fingers or even a twig.

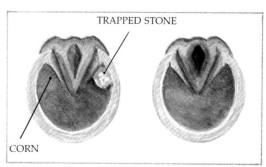

Left: Bruises and corns show as reddish marks; trapped stones are usually fairly obvious. *Right:* Frog infected with thrush.

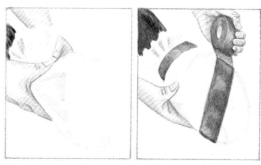

If you do not have an Equiboot or foot bandage, a foot poultice can be held in place by using a plastic bag secured by tape around the hoof.

Lack of care and cleanliness can lead to the development of thrush. The pony on the right is a likely candidate, especially if the feet are rarely picked out.

Laminitis

Laminitis means inflammation of the laminae, the layers of sensitive tissue which lie in the area between the horn and the pedal bone.

There are many causes, from general toxaemia to excessive work on hard ground, but the most common is too much rich food and too little exercise. Laminitis is particularly associated with grass-fed ponies in the late spring and early summer when they tend to gorge on new, lush grass, but it can also arise in any horse at any time of the year if the diet is too heavy for the work load.

The pain of the laminae becoming inflamed has been likened, in human terms, to having heavily swollen feet encased in tight boots. Humans, however, can remove their boots; ponies cannot remove their hooves.

The most obvious sign of laminitis is a tendency for the pony to support its weight on its heels. Since the inflammation *always* starts in the *front* feet, the pony will stand with its front legs thrust forwards and its weight carried on its heels.

Immediate treatment by a vet is essential as the pony must be given relief from the severe pain. Pain-killers or a local anaesthetic could be needed as well as anti-inflammatory drugs. The farrier should also be able to help by paring the feet so that the pressure can be relieved and, later, by fitting special shoes.

If neglected, laminitis leads to permanent damage to the foot, as the pedal bone rotates. Even after a mild bout, the pony will be left with characteristic ridges around the hoof wall and a susceptibility to the disease in future years.

Laminitis will cause your pony to stand like this, front feet thrust forward, weight on the heels. It is essential to bring him in and call the vet.

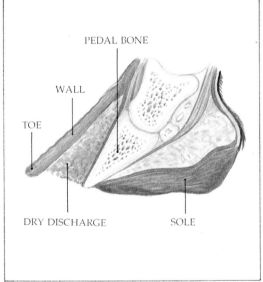

PEDAL BONE

WALL

TOE

DRY DISCHARGE

SOLE

Following a severe attack of laminitis, **discharge** from inflamed laminae pushes the toe outwards. The swivelled pedal bone pierces the sole, which has dropped.